Single Mothers and Living for Christ 3

The Challenges of Parenting

Tréasa Brown

REJOICE
Essential Publishing

Tréasa Brown/Rejoice Essential Publishing

PO BOX 512

Effingham, SC 29541

www.republishing.org

Unless otherwise indicated, scripture is taken from the King James Version.

Single Mothers And Living For Christ 3/ Tréasa Brown

ISBN-13: 978-1-956775-77-8

Dedication

This book is dedicated to my Lord and Savior, Jesus Christ, who inspired me to write this book. I also would like to dedicate this book to my grandmother, Missionary Hazel Lee Hughes, who was an ANOINTED mother of 12 children and to my grandfather, Curtis Hughes Sr. You passed before I was born, but you gave our family foundation on the Word of God! Last, I dedicate this book to all the ANOINTED single mothers all around the globe. Be encouraged. With God, you CAN do this!

Contents

Acknowledgements

Father, Son, and Holy Ghost! Lord, you ALWAYS inspire me and you've been my #1 encouragement. I would be lost without you! I love you Lord!

To my 3 beautiful children, DeVontaé, Julissa, and Julius Steele, mommy loves you; we're going to make it!

To my mother, Hazel Nelson, who has undergirded me, there's so much I could say about you. I love you and thank you for ALL your prayers. You're the jewel in my life!

To my Uncle Joe, you may have passed on, but you have always been like a father figure in my life! Thank you so much, I love you and you're missed! I will still carry you in my heart on this journey with me!

To my Dad, Tommy Lee Brown, I love you and I'm praying for you!

To my siblings, Caémeille Choyce, Tony, and Tyler Brown, I love you all! We have been through a lot together, but God will get the GLORY out of our lives. It's our turn! Make room for God to bless you!

To my future husband, I know you'll be "Taylor-Made by God!" As I always say, it's going to take a special person to fill those shoes. Manifest MOG, that we may do ministry together for the Kingdom! (An act of faith!)

Finally, to all those who encouraged me during the process of writing my third book, thank you so much! It's been a challenge, but I'm still going by God's grace! God bless you! Enjoy!

Tréasa Brown

Foreword

Wisdom is what comes to mind as I read the third part of "Single Mothers and Living for Christ." This book will teach mothers to be patient when raising their children. The devil loves to mess with our children if he can't get to us. He wants to derail their purpose. Prophetess Tréasa Brown does an excellent job exposing the devil's tactics when it comes to parenting. She shares her life experiences of her concerns, victories, and challenges. Through her mentorship and wisdom, we are encouraged to believe God to bless our children to grow up to be men and women of God after the Father's heart. She teaches us how to pray for our children and help them succeed in life. If you feel the stress of parenting, this book will uplift you so you can know that God will turn things around. You will be encouraged to know that you are making a difference in your children's lives and you are valuable. After you finish reading this book, make sure you sow a copy into another mom's life so she too can draw the strength to raise her children in the fear and admonition of the Lord.

Her children arise up, and call her blessed; — Proverbs 31:28

Kimberly Moses
Chief editor and publisher
Rejoice Essential Publishing

Monkey in the Middle

If you've ever played "monkey in the middle" with two friends back in elementary school, you'll remember it was no fun being the one in the middle. The ball was thrown over your head, to keep you from catching it. One would feel like the "odd one out." While playing the game, you'll remember looking in both directions from side to side, strategizing how to catch the ball. Once caught, you switched places with a friend who mistakenly let you catch it. As single Christian mothers, we can feel we're in the middle of a lot, while trying to raise our children, not knowing which direction to turn, or when to go left or right. Unfortunately, parenting NEVER comes with a manual and the enemy, if you will, doesn't want us to "catch it"!

Should I let them go here or there? Do I let them wear this or that? What friendships do I allow them to engage in? (So many questions are running through our minds.) One thing we can be sure of, is to let the Word of God and the Holy Spirit guide us. The Word of God carries instruction and can be a POWERFUL tool to help form guidelines. Without the Lord, we are bound to fail. Later in this book, we will talk about planting the seed and letting the Holy Spirit minister to us concerning it. Though faced with middle ground decisions, there's protocol. The Bible declares, in Proverbs 22:6, "Train up a child in the way he SHOULD GO: And when he is old, he will not depart from it." So many times, we're leaning to our own understanding in the matter. When Proverbs 3:5-7 declares, "Trust in the Lord with ALL thine heart; And lean not unto thine own understanding. In ALL thy ways acknowledge him, And he shall direct thy paths. Be not wise in thine own eyes: Fear the LORD, and depart from evil."

We're trying to go by our own judgment or intellect. What feels good or what SEEMS right. We want to be the "cool parent," instead of the one who seeks out the wisdom of God. We must be careful! Popularity can get us into a great deal of trouble. The hard truth is we're not called to be popular, but rather peculiar.

Keep away from the middle, so you're not easily swayed. It's like how Jesus spoke to the church of the Laodiceans, in Revelation 3:15-16 which declares, "I know thy works, that thou art neither cold nor hot: I would thou wert cold or hot. So then because thou art lukewarm, and neither cold nor hot, I will spue thee out of my mouth." Even our Father doesn't want us lukewarm or somewhere in the middle. It causes confusion! The Bible also declares to us, in James 1:8, "A double minded man is UNSTABLE in all his ways."

I know! This isn't a popular topic for today's society or the new generation, but it must be addressed. How you train up your children, single mothers, will make YOU accountable. They ARE a reflection of us! Do they have to follow in our EXACT footsteps and do everything like us? Of course not! God forbid! Their ultimate example is Jesus, and likewise for us. In fact, the Lord knows the path they're going to take. With discipline in love, much prayer and training, it will suffice. We too, have made MANY mistakes, but we don't have to allow a replica. However, why not make a difference and impact them in a better way? We will have to stand before God and give an answer. I say it often! The Lord has entrusted US with our children! What we deposit into their spirit is vital! (My God) And what they disperse is a representation. Discipline is necessary! Proverbs 29:15 declares, "The rod and reproof give wisdom: But a child left to HIMSELF bringeth his mother to shame."

Of course, you can have fun with your children and be adventurous. But there's a blueprint for the standards you should set for your children and it's through the Word of God. Our children can be caught in the middle too. With the pure pressure of school systems, society, acquaintances and friends, they can be swayed. But looking at the BIGGER picture, it's about life and death. One wrong choice for your child can change everything, especially in today's generation! Most of society runs from and hates the truth!

On the evening of February 17th, 2022, I was compelled to ask my children what peer pressures they have. My oldest son DeVontaé said, "Vaping and hot girls." My daughter Julissa mentioned makeup, clothes and relationships. And Julius, my youngest son said, "School and girls." However, he believed he didn't have many peer pressures. Do you see what I mean? There's nothing new under the sun, but it keeps getting worse with time! I had them expound as to WHY these were some of their peer pressures. I gave them feedback with TRUTH.

Let's look at a familiar story in the Bible, where a prophet named Micaiah is hated for eventually speaking the TRUTH. Let me summarize. There's a king of Judah, by the name of Jehoshaphat and the king of Israel who speaks of going to battle to Ramoth-Gilead. King Jehoshaphat tells the king of Israel to ENQUIRE the Word of the Lord concerning it. All the prophets of Baal lie and tell the king of Israel to "Go up; for the LORD shall deliver it into the hand of the king." 1 Kings 22:7-8 declares, "And Jehoshaphat said, Is there not here a prophet of the LORD besides, that we might enquire of him? And the king of Israel said unto

Jehoshaphat, There is yet ONE man, Micaiah the son of Imlah, by whom we may enquire of the LORD: BUT I HATE HIM; for he doth not prophesy good concerning me, but evil. And Jehoshaphat said, Let not the king say so."

The king of Israel sends for Micaiah the prophet and he tells them, what the Lord tells him, he will speak. But at first, Micaiah prophesys the same thing as the lying prophets of Bail. Finally, Micaiah truly says what thus saith the Lord. Skipping down to verses 16-24, it says, "And the king said unto him, How many times shall I adjure thee that thou tell me nothing but that which is TRUE in the name of the LORD? And he (Micaiah) said, I saw all Israel scattered upon the hills, as sheep that have not a shepherd: and the LORD said, These have no master: let them return every man to his house in peace. And the king of Israel said unto Jehoshaphat, Did I not tell thee that he would prophesy no good concerning me, but evil? And he said, Hear thou therefore the word of the LORD: I saw the LORD sitting on his throne, and all the host of heaven standing by him on his right hand and on his left. And the Lord said, Who shall persuade Ahab, that he may go up and fall at Ramoth-gilead? And one said on this manner, and another said on that manner. And there came forth a spirit, and stood before the LORD, and said, I will persuade him. And the LORD said unto him, Wherewith? And he said, I will go forth, and I will be a LYING SPIRIT in the mouth of ALL his prophets. And he said, Thou shalt persuade him, and prevail also: go forth, and do so. Now therefore, behold, the LORD hath put a LYING SPIRIT in the mouth of all these thy prophets, and the LORD hath spoken evil concerning thee. But Zedekiah the son of Chenaanah went near, and smote Micaiah on the cheek, and said, Which way went the Spirit of the LORD from me to speak unto thee?"

What's your point WOG? You may not be liked but tell the TRUTH! "Monkey in the Middle" was a silly game we played. We can't be caught between two opinions, when it comes to the TRUTH! It's that simple. Why, as parents, do we compromise? Why do we lie to our children? Give them facts and leave no room for the enemy! We are told to give the enemy NO PLACE! Ephesians 4:27 declares, "Neither give place to the devil."

Eli the priest and his sons Hophni and Phinehas, paid a heavy price, to the point of death. Eli's sons caused men to abhor the offerings of the Lord and laid with the women that assembled at the door of the tabernacle of the congregation (See 1 Samuel 2:22). Eli had rebuked his sons for their wrong. However the scripture tells us they DIDN'T HEARKEN to the voice of their father. 1 Samuel 2:12 declares, "Now the sons of Eli were sons of Belial; they knew NOT the LORD." Verse 17 in the first part of that stanza says, "Wherefore the sin of the young men was VERY GREAT before the LORD:" ... Judgment indeed came upon Eli's house (See 1 Samuel 2:22-36).

The Lord is looking at our children as well. My oldest son tells me often, "But mom, I'm not saved," as if it's some excuse to justify his wrong of what he wants to do. As often as it's said, I remind him I have an assignment concerning him. His salvation is a CHOICE! As for me, I will not compromise or be slack concerning my mission! Though Eli warned his sons, the consequences were severe for their hard of hearing and disobedience. Think about it...A parent getting in trouble at the expense of their own child? No thanks! It's worth me telling my children the truth and to help prevent inadequate situations. God gave us authority single mothers and we must utilize it! I'm not saying abuse your authority, but with wisdom, take dominion!

The scripture tells us, "For the wages of sin is death; but the GIFT of God is eternal life through Jesus Christ our Lord (Romans 6:23)." Are we to sugar coat things because they're our own children? Absolutely NOT! Are we learning something about the middle ground? The scripture tells me to let my yes be yes and my no be no. Matthew 5:37 declares, "But let your communication be Yea, yea; Nay, nay: for whatsoever is more than these cometh of evil." Help us God.

Decide to be the parent and mother, that God is calling you to be in this hour. Take authority! Protect your seed and don't give into the adversary because of what the world is doing. Be kingdom minded! Our children are precious and a gift from the Lord. Let us be sober and let the Lord lead us into all truth for this new generation. No more middle ground. Pick a side!

Planting the Seed!

One thing about sowing seeds, is they must fall on good ground. Jesus gave the best example through a parable concerning sowing seed (See Matthew 13:3-9). In those verses, Jesus talks about the Sower and where the seeds fell. Some fell by the wayside and the birds devoured them. Some fell on stony places, were scourged by the sun, had no root and withered away. But then others fell on good ground and brought forth fruit. The Bible says some a hundredfold, some sixtyfold and some thirtyfold. Christ is the Sower and as His children, we are to spread the gospel, His Word!

One thing I learned in the natural, it matters how the seed is planted. Good soil is key, and it must be ready to receive seed. I thought that was POWERFUL, thinking about it on a spiritual level!

Look at it this way, the soil of our hearts must be prepared to receive seed (God's Word). We want it to fall on good ground. In the natural, we want the seed planted in the right position so that the roots can grow properly. The depth and how far apart you sow your seeds are also factors. (The root of a thing is important) Interesting! After the seed has properly been planted, you look for signs of germination. Germination is defined as the development of a plant from a seed or spore after a period of dormancy. Or the process of something coming into existence and developing.

How important are our children's growth and development and what seeds are we as single mothers, planting? Excuse me for being the odd mother out, but we're so focused on their natural growth that we forget their spiritual development. We say things like, "Kids will be kids," or "They're just being a kid," yet I see children being used mightily for God. Some are filled with the Holy Spirit, preaching, prophesying etc.... and yet we make excuses for our own. Sure, it's a choice our children must make, in wanting to serve God, but what are we planting in the meantime? They're not JUST a kid. There's more! They're anointed, chosen and God has HIS HAND upon their lives! We will talk about covering their anointing in the next chapter. Here's an example of why you must see BEYOND this concept. On June 18th, 2012, I believe the Lord spoke these words to me concerning my children.

"My hand is upon your children's lives....
They will be blessed because of you...
They are called...
They belong to me...
They will be blessed" ...

I was a babe in Christ when I received this word, but you get the concept! God was telling me directly about my own seed. He cares! In addition, last month in the "Advanced School of the Prophets," Prophetess Leslie Harvey released a word over my life. God spoke through her and said, "Prophetess Tréasa, I see your entire household operating in the prophetic. You have a prophetic home" ... This was not the entire word, but it explained the warfare at different moments. We, as parents, must put up a spiritual fight for our children! This is a spiritual battle!

Are we truly doing all we can to tell them about Jesus? Or do we keep putting it off and over to the side? For how long? All because, in your eyes, they're JUST a kid? At least TEACH them! David said it best when he declared, Thy WORD have I hid in mine heart, that I might NOT sin against thee (Psalm 119:11). Do we think the Word of God is for adults ONLY? Are we doubting God can raise our seed? Think about it. Why do we shy away from it? It's something to think about!

I have a problem with pushing our children's spiritual well fare off and telling ourselves, "They'll get there." You, single mothers, women of God, are planted in their lives for a reason. God raised you up to instill! He's chosen YOU as a vessel to pour into your child or children. God wants to use them! The Bible declares in Matthew 19:14, "But Jesus said, Suffer little children, and forbid them not, to come unto me: for of such IS the kingdom of heaven."

In the past, I've often felt the Word of God I was teaching was going over my children's heads. But the more I listened to them speak, pray, or sing around the house, I knew the seed had been planted. But what about their early teenage stages? (Whew!) I'm in those stages currently and it's NOT easy. It seems the older they get, the further they run from the Word. But STILL, I press because I have an assignment! If you can't tell already single mothers, I'm very passionate about this!

I know this may sound cliché, but as we deposit the Word, it will stay with them, no matter the circumstances. Our job is vital and it's to plant the seed! (I feel the Lord encouraging ME right now). Proverbs 22:6, as we know it declares, "TRAIN UP a child in the way he should go: and when he is old, he will not depart from it." The training is NECESSARY and sowing the seed is a part of it.

As single mothers, we must understand this ONE thing. Our FIRST ministry is indeed to our home and if we're neglecting it, what will it speak of us? Listen, Proverbs 14:1 declares, "EVERY wise woman buildeth her house: but the foolish plucketh it down with her hands." In addition, 1 Timothy 3:4-5 declares, "One that ruleth well his OWN house, having his CHILDREN in subjection with all gravity; (For if a man know not how to rule HIS OWN house, HOW shall he take care of the church of God?)" This is straight forward! If you can't rule your house, how will you take care of God's work? You can't! It's that simple and you'd be out of order. Planting the seed isn't always easy, but someone must plant it! Single mothers, let it begin with you! I'll never forget when I was praying in my mother's prayer closet one day and the Lord, I believe showed me a small inner vision. I saw a big hand of a Gardner, planting in the garden. It was interesting!

A Gardner is one who tends and cultivates! One who cares for and nurtures! Plant the seed single mothers and don't let anyone tell you otherwise. I've learned the enemy will try to rob them of what's already been planted, while having them deposit other things in their spirit. If your seed means anything to you, you'll do whatever it takes to help their growth, but in the RIGHT way. PLANT THE SEED! I leave you with Genesis 17:7 which declares, "And I will "ESTABLISH" my covenant between me and thee and THY SEED after thee in their generations for an everlasting covenant, to be a God unto thee, and to thy seed after thee."

Covering Their Anointing

There are a few words in definition, I would like to disclose on COVER. The definitions are as follows:

1. To conceal, by an intervening object.
2. Clothe, as to cover with a robe or mantle.
3. To shelter, protect and defend.
4. To refrain from disclosing, or veil.

This is so important when it comes to our child or children. We must understand it's MUCH bigger than them. It's about their anointing! When you become a covering to your children, you set up God's divine hedge of protection! You're signaling to the adversary, that beyond THIS POINT, you're blocked! Why? Because you've APPLIED the blood of Jesus! Prayer has been your weapon! This isn't to say difficulties won't come up against our seed, but it does imply it won't prosper! Isaiah 54:17, in the first part of that stanza, declares, "No weapon that is formed against thee shall prosper."

You see, the blood of Jesus is your DEFENSE, your ally when the enemy revolts against you! When the BLOOD covers you, you're more than capable of covering them! Psalm 94:22 declares, "But the LORD is my defense; and my God is the rock of my refuge." Cover your babies DAILY and don't let up for anything!

An anointing is given by God! It means to smear or rub with oil, set apart, or consecrate. Single mothers, it's imperative to anoint our seed! As a woman of God, I know the Lord has revealed to me that my children are anointed! Therefore, we must be like a forcefield in the spirit, WAGING WAR against the adversary over them! We must NOT hand our children over to the world and let the enemy make ruin of them! Play days are OVER concerning this matter! We can't afford to get off assignment covering them.

I would like to show you three different examples in scripture, where Jesus, John the Baptist and Samuel were chosen, anointed at YOUNG ages. Luke 1:31-33 declares, "And, behold, thou shalt conceive in thy womb, and bring forth a son, and shalt call his name JESUS. He shall be great, and shall be called the Son of the Highest: and the Lord God shall give unto him the throne of his father David: And he shall reign over the house of Jacob for ever; and of his kingdom there shall be no end." Luke 2:34 declares, "And Simeon blessed them, and said unto Mary his mother, Behold, THIS CHILD is set for the fall and rising again of many in Israel; and for a SIGN which shall be spoken against;" (Powerful prophecies over Jesus) verse 40, "And the CHILD grew, and waxed strong in SPIRIT, filled with WISDOM: and the GRACE of God was upon him."

Jesus did something profound at age 12. Let's re-fresh our memory. In that same chapter, verses 42-52 reads, "And when he was twelve years old, they went up to Jerusalem after the custom of the feast. And when they had fulfilled the days, as they returned, the CHILD JESUS tarried behind in Jerusalem; and Joseph and his mother knew not of it. But they, sup-posing him to have been in the company, went a day's journey; and they sought him among their kinsfolk and acquaintance. And when they found him not, they turned back again to Jerusalem, seeking him. And it came to pass, that after three days they found him in the temple, sitting in the midst of the DOCTORS, both hearing them, and asking them questions. And ALL that heard him were astonished at his understand-ing and answers. And when they saw him, they were AMAZED: and his mother said unto him, Son, why hast thou thus dealt with us? behold, thy father and I have sought thee sorrowing. And he said unto them, How is it that ye sought me? wist ye not that I must be about my Father's business?" Verse 52 declares, "And Jesus INCREASED in wisdom and stature, and in favour with God and man."

Many were amazed at Jesus, by age 12! He was destined to be the Savior of the WHOLE WORLD! Next, John the Baptist. Luke 1:15-16 says, "For he shall be great in the sight of the Lord, and shall drink neither wine nor strong drink; and he shall be FILLED with the Holy Ghost, even from his mother's womb. And MANY of the children of Israel shall he turn to the Lord their God." Verse 80, "And the CHILD Samuel grew on, and waxed STRONG IN SPIRIT, and was in the deserts till the day of his shewing unto Israel." Can you imagine, a CHILD being filled with the Holy Ghost from his mother's womb? That's profound! Chosen and destined for greatness!

Last, but certainly not least, Samuel. 1 Samuel 2:18-19 declares, "But Samuel ministered before the LORD, being A CHILD, girded with a linen ephod. Moreover his mother made him a little coat, and brought it to him from year to year, when she came up with her husband to offer the yearly sacrifice." Verse 26, "And the CHILD Samuel grew on, and was IN FAVOR both with the LORD, and also with men." 1 Samuel 3:1 also declares, "And the CHILD Samuel ministered unto the LORD before Eli. And the word of the LORD was precious in those days; there was no open vision." Briefly summarizing Samuel chapter 3, as a CHILD, Samuel begins to hear a voice speaking to him, while laid down to sleep. It was the LORD, which called out to him not once, but three times. Though Samuel thought it was Eli, Eli the priest perceived it was the Lord. He told the child Samuel to say, "Speak, LORD, for thy servant heareth" ... (See 1 Samuel 3-10). Verse 7 declares, "Now Samuel did not yet KNOW the LORD, neither was the word of the LORD REVEALED unto him." Though he was a CHILD, God began to reveal Himself to Samuel, because he would be a CHOSEN vessel unto the Lord. 1 Samuel 3:19-20 declares, "And Samuel grew, and the LORD was with him, and did let NONE of his words fall to the ground. And ALL ISRAEL from Dan even to Beer-sheba knew that Samuel was established to be a prophet of the LORD."

Single mothers, I'm pointing out these examples in scripture, so you'll remember God has a plan for our children too! These are reminders that God wants to use our seed. He wants them to grow in HIM! Are we guarding our children's anointing or letting them dabble in any and everything? Therefore, different attacks can prowl their way towards our seed.

Unexpected attacks which can't be explained. The enemy knows there's an anointing on their lives as well and therefore, he won't WAIT until they're older. How do you know this WOG? Just look at the school shootings around the world. Suicides, identity issues, and confusion surround our children.

According to the National Institute of Mental Health, most child suicide deaths occurred in the home at 95.5%: 65.6% in the bedroom, 78.4% by hanging, and 18.7% with a firearm. 58.4% is stated that a parent was indeed at home, during the child's death. If we, as parents, would pour into our children and tell them WHO they are in God, the enemy would have no room nor access to leave them confused about their worth or identity! Our babies need to know their purpose and that GOD has a plan for their lives! No one knows your child better than you do, except our GREAT GOD!

The truth is our children are seeking their identity in the wrong things and deceptive influences (People with wrong motives). They're MASKED because of this. I had this conversation with my children already. When they're trying to be something they're

NOT, due to the wrong influences. It's fake! We often hear the saying, "Fake it until you make it!" We know that's deceptive. It's a lie! There are pressures on our children with school systems, acquaintances and friends, which teach the opposite of what we're instilling. We're not ignorant to it! In fact, we see it all around us, right in our faces BOLDLY. It's teaching our children to rebel and be disobedient! The question is, what can we do about it? PRAY! Continue to cover their anointing.

Society is starting to have more of an influence on our children than we do. Why do you think that is? I believe it's because we're not spending enough time POURING into our children, ministering to their spirit, building them up, taking our own hands and anointing them, and declaring and decreeing over them, what GOD SAID and NOT what we see the enemy doing! (This is ministering to me right now) We're letting someone else do the work when it should be us! We've become lazy and reverted to "kids will be kids." The devil is a liar!

Single mothers, let's get our authority back, which God gave us! There's POWER in our mouths! Job

22:28 declares, "Thou shalt also DECREE a thing, and it SHALL be established unto thee: And the light shall shine upon thy ways." (I literally feel the presence of God right here as I'm writing. There are tears filling my eyes!) Let's speak the Word of God over our children! As a matter of fact, when you hear your children speaking something contrary to what GOD said about their life, rebuke it and replace it with what HE said! Listen carefully to what your children are decreeing over their lives. I've learned this and discovered to pay CLOSE attention to what they're speaking in the atmosphere. My children are often rebuked at times, especially if I hear something negative spoken. I do my best to replace it with God's Word and build them UP! Sometimes they can degrade themselves based on what they heard someone else say. I do my best to not allow room for it!

Children are like a sponge. They absorb. We must make note and be serious about what's declared over them. If we love them, we'll speak life over them. If you don't get anything else out of what I said in this chapter, please understand your child is anointed! They have an anointing upon their life that needs to be cultivated, nurtured, and covered! Stay on your post and let God be God!

Surrender Them to God

"Surrendering them to me, means you understand that you don't own the rights to their life. You understand that they are my creation, my invention. Their mine says the Lord, therefore you must bring them to me like a sacrifice. Remember Abraham? He stopped at nothing to bring Isaac to me...His one and only son whom he loved. But he understood sacrifice...Their mine...They belong to me."

Wow! God uttered those words to me right at the beginning of this chapter. It began to flow. If the Lord will take His time to minister these specific words about children, why would we think any less of our children? If God cares, you should care! We need the HEART OF GOD! In the prophetic word He uttered, God highlighted Abraham sacrificing his son Isaac. Genesis 22:2 declares, "And he said, Take now thy son, thine only son Isaac, whom thou lovest, and get thee into the land of Moriah; and offer him there for a burnt offering upon one of the mountains which I will tell thee of."

We know Abraham also had Ishmael, which God also blessed. Genesis 17: 20-21 declares, "And as for Ishmael, I have heard thee: Behold, I have blessed him, and will make him fruitful, and will multiply him exceedingly; twelve princes shall he beget, and I will make him a great nation. But my covenant will I establish with Isaac, which Sarah shall bear unto thee at this set time in the next year." ISAAC was his one and only son which the covenant would be ESTABLISHED! Let's look at three other scriptures that authenticates this. Genesis 21:12 declares, "And God said unto Abraham, Let it not be grievous in thy sight because of the lad, and because of thy bond-woman; in all that Sarah hath said unto thee, hearken unto her voice; for IN ISAAC shall thy seed be called." (That bondwoman was Ishmael's mother Hagar and the lad mentioned was Ishmael). Romans 9:6-7 says, "Not as though the word of God hath taken none effect. For they are not all Israel, which are of Israel: Neither, because they are the seed of Abraham, are they all children: but, IN ISAAC shall thy seed be called." Hebrews 11:18, "Of whom it was said, That IN ISAAC shall thy seed be called:"

In three different scriptures and three different books, God spoke it and He meant it! A Biblical definition of surrender can be defined as to yield to the power of another; to give or deliver up possession, deliver unto, to give over. If we are honest, surrendering is not always easy because we know SACRIFICE is involved. Let me give you an example. Hannah asked for "a man child" (Samuel) and said she would give him back to the Lord all the days of his life. 1 Samuel 1:11 declares, "And she vowed a vow, and said, O LORD of hosts, if thou wilt indeed look on the affliction of thine handmaid, and remember me, and not forget thine handmaid, but wilt give unto thine handmaid a man child, then I will give him unto the LORD all the days of his life, and there shall no razor come upon his head."

What do you mean woman of God? Dedicate your children to the Lord, present them before Him in prayer, as a SIGN that you will allow God to use them for HIS SERVICE and for HIS GLORY! I too, dedicated my children back to the Lord. This part of the challenge means you'll take on the responsibility of reminding your children who God is in their life. Refresh their memory! They can't partake in what everyone else partakes in. They can't go where they want to go. They're different. God's hand is upon their lives, and they will always stand out from the crowd. Speak to every gift in your child, knowing their gifts are meant to be used to glorify the Father!

Some of you may be thinking, "This seems like too much woman of God!" It's quite the responsibility, but worth it! Think of it as, I'm protecting my child. I've learned it's difficult to surrender specific things to God about your children because as parents, we want to put our hands in the situation. Psalm 46:10, in the first part of that stanza declares to us, "Be STILL and know that I am God:" ...In Exodus 14:13, we see Moses tell the children of Israel "Fear ye not, stand still, and see the salvation of the Lord."

If you're like me, single mothers, you understand there's moments when you worry about the future. There's times concern sets in. An INFLUX of thoughts and questions race through the mind about our children, making it overwhelming! Have you ever questioned if you're doing enough for them as a single mom? This is tough, but it's where surrender comes in at. Where we miss the mark in raising our children, (because there will be mistakes made) You must trust that GOD will make up the difference. Keep in mind the Word of God MUST be the foundation of everything you do! Build your house! (Remember Proverbs 14:1).

Sometimes we, as mothers, can feel so depleted working with our children. We feel as though we've done all we can do. But Ephesians 6:10 declares, "Finally, my brethren, be strong in the Lord, and in the power of his might." We, as single mothers, certainly can't do this in our own strength. We try to be Super Woman! Zechariah 4:6 declares, "Then he ANSWERED and spake unto me, saying, This is the word of the LORD unto Zerubbabel, saying, Not by might, nor by power, but by my spirit, saith the LORD of hosts." We need the Lord to help us! We need the Spirit of the Lord to dwell on the inside of us, so we can have the wisdom of God in how to proceed in surrender.

Sure, the Lord wants us to teach and train our children with His help. However, I'm learning as a mother, there are situations beyond my control as a mother, and I MUST surrender it to the Lord. He has the final say over my children and their destiny! As I obey the divine instructions given to me by the Lord for my children, the rest is up to Him. Only He can soften the hearts of our children. Only He can touch their minds! As I live a Holy lifestyle to the best of my knowledge before them, I surrender the rest to Almighty God!

If you're feeling jammed and don't know what else to do, turn it over to Jesus. SURRENDER! A woman of God named Prophetess Trinae once told me in a nutshell, (paraphrasing) I can't make my children choose the Lord. It's not on me! They must choose for themselves. Perhaps I wasn't aware that as I teach my children the things of God, I feel it's on me. Why? Sometimes, things go another way. I have no control over this, but I do have authority in how I discipline and teach them. The rest, I will learn to surrender to God. As I encourage myself at this moment, I encourage you single mothers. Let the Lord lead you and the rest, leave it in the Master's hand. Let's show Him we surrender!

Transitioning

The sweet memories I have of my children: in my womb, as a newborn, toddler years, young children, to older children. Now, we're at tween to young teen years. (Whew) Remember the "Happy little accidents," with such innocence of a child having their first birthday cake, with chocolate or vanilla icing smudged on their face? Now it turns into the huge messes around the house and you are reminding them to complete their chores. How do we adjust? Transition is constantly happening daily throughout life. It's defined as the process or period of changing from one state or condition to another. Single mothers, there's other protocols that must be exercised as our children transition from one age to the next. What do you mean? While there's a sure foundation that we know to be true, (the Word of God) we can be sure the way we approached one issue before won't be the same approach with another. All done with love in mind, discipline is still the order of the day!

How do we deal with the transitions? The WISDOM of God! James 1:5 declares, "If any of you lack wisdom, let him ask of God, that giveth to all men liberally, and upbraideth not; and it shall be given him." With different stages as a single mom, I'm learning I must ask the Father for His Wisdom! As our children begin to mature, they're exposed to different environments, they struggle with different issues and face certain giants. When a transition takes place, it usually affects everyone in the home.

Keeping the Word of God at the forefront is vital, but one thing I've noticed, for many of us, our children resist. There's warfare and attacks that come. The methods used for teaching the Word of God when smaller, shifts as they become older. WISDOM must be applied! Pin for thought. Ultimately, we want their soul to be won to Christ! Proverbs 11:30 declares, "The fruit of the righteous is a tree of life; And he that winneth souls is wise." It may not be us that lead them to give their life to Christ, but our lives are still on display before them.

We're still talking about transition! It's just like us as sons and daughters in the Body of Christ. We cannot stay on spiritual milk forever. With time, consistency, and dedication, we graduate to spiritual meat in the Word. 1 Peter 2:2 declares, "As newborn babes, desire the sincere milk of the word, that ye may grow thereby." In addition, 1 Corinthians 3:2 says, "I have fed you with milk, and not with meat: for hitherto ye were not able to bear it, neither yet now are ye able." We want to graduate to meat!

Look at Jesus' transfiguration! Even He didn't remain the same. Matthew 17:1-2 declares, "And after six days Jesus taketh Peter, James, and John his brother, and bringeth them up into an high mountain apart, and was TRANSFIGURED before them: and his face did shine as the sun, and his raiment was white as the light." Luke 9:28-29 also says, "And it came to pass about eight days after these sayings, he took Peter and John and James, and went up into a mountain to pray. And as he prayed, the fashion of his countenance was ALTERED, and his raiment was white and glistering." While in transition, may our hearts, minds and spirits be transfigured, in Jesus' name! We will need it!

Once we've taught and raised our children on the foundation of the Word of God, somewhere along the line, THEY must bring forth application. As said, "One plants, one waters, but God gives the increase!" Glory To God! Still, they will have to choose right from wrong and be the ones to resist the devil, that he may flee! What a transition to take your hands off. Therefore, it's so vital to have the Holy Spirit IN US, that we may know how to approach the transition we're facing. Holy Spirit can direct into all truth and give us divine instruction for our children.

If you don't catch anything else I've said, please understand though transition is taking place in their lives, the foundation remains the same! For example, in my children's tween to young teen years, I thought things would get easier. But if I can be very transparent with you, it became challenging. Most adolescents, but not all, feel as though they can do what they will. TRANSITION!

It's as if they feel entitled to their ways. Can I help us single mothers? Stand your ground! What I am saying, is walk in the rightful charge God gave you! Just because a child is transitioning doesn't mean do as they please. Sure, they get privileges with age, but we don't want anything misconstrued.

I'll be transparent. My son, who is now 15, had some "friends" (I call them acquaintances) who needed to be cut off! Note, when you watch your child transition into something they're not, it raises concern. You can see the red flags. Don't ignore them! Their countenance changes: the way they do things, their expressions and even with what they say. Take note and pay attention!

I told my son to stay in the Word, to pray, to drop some friends, to stay focused on his schoolwork and that if he didn't heed the warning through me, God was going to REBUKE him publicly. To make a long story short, a Woman of God named Mother Graham and her husband came into town. She's never met my son or spoken to us in person. God began to speak through her. She spoke almost verbatim, what I told my son in private, and his rebuke was in the open.

This wasn't to embarrass my son, but I believe the wheels began to turn in his head. God caught his attention! Though he's transitioning in age, he will STILL need God and his protection. I was so grateful! Sometimes it takes hearing it from someone else to get the point across to our children. As they transition, we are too. Adjustments must be made, but in moderation. You can't give up on speaking the Word of the Lord over them, simply because you believe they don't want to hear it, because of their age, or because people say, "You're forcing it on them." The devil is a liar! "I hear the song in my head by Lee Williams and the Spiritual QC's, "I Can't Give Up" ... Remember, you have an assignment from Almighty God! Instill it in them!

Stay strong through the transition. As I can attest, it's like a roller coaster ride! So many bumps and unexpected turns. But if we stick with the truth, the battle's already won, no matter what it looks like. The Lord had to bring me back to the basics with my children. Again, this let me know, the foundation is to remain the same. Malachi 3:6 in the first part of that stanza declares, "For I am the LORD, I change not;" … I'm the mother you'll find reading and teaching the Word of God to my children. Only to remember my FIRST ministry is to my home. Teaching them to pray before talking to anyone else because God is FIRST or vice versa. Them reading to me as I listen. God had to remind me to keep it going, no matter the age. Remember, it's ok to transition, but with the wisdom of God, keep the solid foundation!

Social Media

"Global Social Media Statistics" show there are 4.70 billion social media users around the world. That's 50 percent total globally. With approximately 227 million new users joining social media, this time last year. Man! We know there's pros and cons to social media. Such as, being able to connect with family from long distances and seeing people's faces immediately while face timing. Or having meetings with a click of a button, launching ministries, quick access, reaching others clear across the country, you name it, it's on the media. That's profound! Technology has certainly come a long way. Daniel 12:4 declares, "But thou, O Daniel, shut up the words, and seal the book, even to the time of the end: many shall run to and fro, and knowledge shall be increased." There's definitely NOTHING new under the sun. It's in the Word of God.

What about the cons? Destroying self-image and level of confidence. Cyber bullying leading to suicide, dating sites that can lead to disaster, predators with wrong motives, pornography, seductive photos and flat-out distractions. This was off the top of my head! We witness so much in a day's time on the media and God knows them all. My question is how do we utilize it while keeping ourselves and our children focused on the things of God? How do we regulate it? It's in one word, PRIORITIZE! When our children know more explicit lyrics than quoting scripture, we have a problem! We ourselves can get hindered while trying to carry out the work of the Lord. We need balance and some of us need deliverance from what's being deposited in our spirits. Our spirits need a break!

Single mothers, it's important we check in on our children while using the media. As this can open the WRONG doors and portals to a child's soul, spirit, mind, and emotions. Likewise, for us. This instant access has torn families apart, destroyed marriages, ministries, friendships and the list continues. Yes, I know! It's also connected us to healthy relationships, resources, ministries even marriages. It's all in HOW we use the media. As a mother, I've noticed different effects on my seed: in their habits, style, speech, thoughts, self-image, etc....

I believe the media can't be mishandled or underestimated. The media should be regulated as far as how much time our children can spend on it. Have you noticed basic skills have been hindered over the years? Children have lost their handwriting skills, can't sign their name due to electronic signatures, or can't look up a word in the dictionary book? Adults too! I've asked my kids, "What are you going to do if the media shuts down?" What will you know how to do? Perhaps it's important to go back to teaching generation z, how to utilize their hands more and the importance of labor without the "Click of a button." Single mothers, you may say, "We live in a different world now." Or "Everything is digital." This is true, but it wouldn't hurt to teach our children the importance of what they have or how to appreciate privileges. Jeremiah

6:16 declares, "Thus saith the LORD, Stand ye in the ways, and see and ask for the OLD PATHS, where is the GOOD WAY, and walk therein, and ye shall find rest for your souls. But they said, We WILL NOT walk therein."

Have we gone too far with social media? When do we draw the line for our children and ourselves? This is serious! I know this is controversial, but someone must talk about it. Let us have balance before the media becomes our god. The Lord WON'T take second place! Sure, we can use the media where God can be glorified, but for MANY, it's gone another way and has destroyed their life, relationship and walk with God! Revelation 2:5, Jesus declares, "Remember therefore from whence thou are FALLEN, and REPENT, and do the FIRST WORKS; or else I will come unto thee quickly, and will remove thy candlestick out of his place, except thou REPENT."

We must go back to teaching about fasting, reading, and prayer! The JUST shall live by faith (See Romans 1:17, second stanza). Let us be wise single mothers. Haggai 1:5 declares, "Thus saith the LORD of hosts; Consider your ways." Lord help us and our children to keep YOU FIRST and not allow the media to stand in place of our relationship with you, in Jesus' name, amen!

Who They Really Are! (Declarations)

I decree and declare, my children are peace makers, in the mighty name of Jesus, according to Matthew 5:9 which declares, "Blessed are the peacemakers: for they shall be called the children of God."

I decree and declare, my children are humble and will be great, in the name of Jesus, according to Matthew 18:4 which declares, "Whosoever therefore shall humble himself as this little child, the same is greatest in the Kingdom of heaven."

I decree and declare, my children will walk in obedience, in the mighty name of Jesus, according to Colossians 3:20 which declares, "Children, obey your parents in all things: for this is well pleasing unto the Lord."

I decree and declare, no one will withhold my children from coming to the Lord, in the name of Jesus, according to Matthew 19:14 which declares, "But Jesus said, "Suffer little children, and forbid them not, to come unto me: for such is the kingdom of heaven."

I decree and declare, that no man will despise their youth and they will be an example to others, in the mighty name of Jesus, according to 1 Timothy 4:12, "Let no man despise thy youth; but be thou an example of the believers, in word, in conversation, in charity, in spirit, in faith, in purity."

I decree and declare, that not only will my children obey, but they will honor both father and mother, that it may be well with them, and they may live long upon the earth, in the name of Jesus. Ephesians 6:1-3 declares, "Children, obey your parents in the Lord: for this is right. Honor thy father and mother; which is the first commandment with promise; That it may be well with thee, and thou mayest live long on the earth."

I decree and declare, my children will hear and follow instructions, in the Mighty name of Jesus, according to Proverbs 1:8-9 which declares, "My son hear the instructions of thy father, and forsake not the law of thy mother: For they shall be an ornament of grace unto thy head, and chains about thy neck."

I decree and declare, my children are a heritage of the Lord, and the fruit of the womb is their reward, in the name of Jesus. Psalm 127:3 declares, "Lo, children are an heritage of the LORD: and the fruit of the womb is his reward."

I decree and declare, my children are created in the image of God, in the Mighty name of Jesus, according to Genesis 1:27, which declares, "So God created man in his own image, in the image of God created he him; male and female created he them."

I decree and declare, my children will listen, and I will teach them the fear of the Lord, in the name of Jesus, according to Psalm 34:11 which declares, "Come, ye children, hearken unto me: I will teach you the fear of the LORD."

I decree and declare, my children can do all things through Christ, which strengthens them, in the mighty name of Jesus, according to Philippians 4:13 which declares, "I can do all things through Christ which strengtheneth me."

I decree and declare, my children will know the thoughts you think towards them Lord, thoughts of peace and not of evil, to given them an expected end, in the Mighty name of Jesus, according to Jeremiah 29:11.

I decree and declare my children will learn to trust in the Lord with all their heart and won't lean to their own understanding. They will acknowledge God in all their ways, and He'll direct their paths, in the name of Jesus, according to Proverbs 3:5.

While writing these declarations, I realize I should be speaking and praying the Word over my children daily. I do pray over them, but it's the Word of God that makes all the difference. Sometimes we can pray amiss. We may not see what the Lord sees in our children right away, but we should ask the Father to show us in the Spirit. They're certainly not what the world portrays them as. They're much greater than that! In a later chapter, we'll talk about "Me against the world?" I'm learning to declare what I want to see in them by HIS WORD! They ARE who the Master says. Declare and decree it with YOUR MOUTH!

The Lies

The importance of telling the truth is priceless! You know how people believe those little white lies won't hurt anyone, or it's ok to tell them? WRONG! A lie is a lie! There's a seed, a root to telling lies and it's the adversary himself! The Bible declares in John 8:44, "Ye are of your father the devil, and the lusts of your father ye will do. He was a murderer from the BEGINNING, and abode not in the truth, because there is NO TRUTH in him. When he speaketh a lie, he speaketh of his own: for he is a LIAR, and the father of it." Jesus Himself told us, He IS the way, the TRUTH and the life, according to John 14:6. Rejecting the truth is like rejecting Jesus Himself. We must teach and stand on the authentic truth, when pouring into our children. I've always asked the Lord to tell me the truth, even if it hurts. Those words carry weight but have value.

Let me give you some examples and actual experiences in my life. Parents have told their children about the tooth fairy when they lose a tooth right? They'll receive money under their pillow in return, when they leave the tooth there. Many parents mean no harm, but they were wrong. Parents know they're the ones taking the tooth and leaving the money.

When I was younger, I caught one of my parents in action, but I pretended to stay asleep because I didn't want them to know I KNEW. When my tooth was placed under my pillow, I remember someone coming into my room. They reached under my pillow, took the tooth and replaced it with money. It was awkward, but I kept it to myself until I became older. Interesting thing is, I only caught it one time throughout my childhood. But I always say, it's like the Lord meant for me to see it.

We are excited around the Christmas Holiday season, which can be VERY controversial! When I was a little girl, I remember believing in Santa Claus. Though there was a real man named St. Nicholas, who was said to hand out toys to children. We know Santa Claus is not real and doesn't hand out toys all over the world. Nothing wrong with the spirit of giving. I'll get back to this in a minute.

In continuing, one year I wrote a letter, and stuck it in the Christmas tree. My brother did the same thing and we believed he received a response from Santa Claus himself. So, I thought the same! I indeed received a letter back and I was that excited little girl! When I became older, I realized the writing was indeed Daddy Choyce's. I remember how distinct his writing was. It was like a replay in my mind of what the writing in the letter looked like. I made a connection that it wasn't Santa.

Going back to Santa Claus giving gifts all over the world, I realized the truth in my young adult years. Then one day, it really hit me! I became sad, knowing no one truly receives gifts on Christmas day from this figure of our imagination, "Santa Claus" or like "tradition" portrays. It hurt! Knowing this truth, I still wrote on gifts like many other parents, "From: Santa," to my children. However, when I gave my life to Christ, I realized this was indeed a lie and I decided I would tell my babies the truth from that point on.

Think about it. Children really BELIEVE! And even better if they believe in Christ our Lord! Matthew 18:6, Jesus declares, "But whoso shall offend one of these little ones which believe in me, it were better for him that a millstone were hanged about his neck, and that he were drowned in the depth of the sea." (Whew!) Weighty and serious! The reason I want to highlight a child's belief, is so we understand how real it is. I want to share my experience. You can damage and hurt them, all because you hold back the truth, even if you mean well.

I volunteered in my daughter Julissa's class, back when she was in kindergarten. It was around the Christmas Holiday during class and one of her good friends was found in a conversation. I couldn't help over hearing. She was in a situation where she was arguing with two other peers in class about Santa Claus.

The boys were telling her Santa Claus wasn't real. I remember somehow getting lured into the conversation and I mentioned how I, Ms. Brown, would tell the truth. In a sweet innocent voice, Julissa's friend said to me, "What is the truth, Ms. Brown?" I basically broke it down to her that Santa Claus wasn't real. She had even mentioned the cookies and milk being drank and eaten. I explained it was her parents.

I'll never forget her face and how she cried in class. Her face was red, with such innocent tears streaming down her cheeks. (She was bawling her eyes out!) This young lady came back to me a year later and explained how she spoke with her parents about it. I was shocked! The impact we have on our children can be for better or for worse, but it matters! I was told I should've let her parents tell her, but I don't believe it's coincidental I was there. I did what was right! It was like a divine setup for me to be there and speak the truth.

Many may not like what I've said on the matter, but it's the truth. We must stop hurting the people we love with lies and build a solid foundation ON TRUTH! We all are being challenged, including me! There are so many other myths told to our children that if we don't become new trend setters, we'll leave them confused. And God is certainly not the author of confusion. 1 Corinthians 14:33 declares, "For God is not the author of confusion, but of peace, as in all churches of saints." Wisdom is the application. Let's not follow traditions and trends because it sounds and looks good single mothers but let's be about truth!

The reality? It may hurt telling your child the truth and you may be thinking, "What's the fun in that?" "I want to keep the imagination alive!" But your kiddos will appreciate you later and thank you for the truth. There are other ways to make things fun without falsehood attached. Are you willing to start a fresh and give up the lies? Perhaps some of you have kids who are older now and have figured it out by now. Maybe it never affected them. Good! But would you do it differently if you could? Or would you have kept it the same? Jesus loved us so much; He gave us truth! He knew we would need it and there would be friction between flesh and spirit. Now that we know better, we can do better. Maybe it makes no difference to you, but I thank God for no more lies!

Me Against the World?

I know it's a "figure of speech," but have you ever felt like the weight of the world was on your shoulders? What do you mean WOG? Feeling overwhelmed, heavy, like all odds are against you? Distraught, deterred, dysfunctional, unable to unwind, unrest? These came to mind right off the top. I recall memorable times, when God allowed me to feel how specific things grieve Him. It was an overwhelming heaviness that made me cry out from the depths of my soul. The first example, when COVID-19 hit, I was interceding between the hours of 12:00 am - 4:00 am. Random people and the Body of Christ began to come before me. I cried out from the depths of my soul, bawling my eyes out. I too, believe I was interceding for the world. God began to speak to me about what He was allowing me to feel. My eyes were so puffy and red afterwards. I felt like I hadn't slept.

Here's what I documented: Monday, May 4th, 2020, "Around 2:33 am, been crying a while." "Cried earlier, went to sleep, got up and cried again." "Oh, how I grieve daughter" ... (Second time around that I cried for hours with the region, people and the Body in mind...All I can say is Lord, we're sorry. Lord, I'm sorry). (The time is usually between the hours of 12:00 am - 4:00 am.) Also, I keep saying help us Lord, as I listened to Dappy T Key's Instrumentals. His music makes me want to worship...And cry before the presence of the Lord...(Grieve) I have been crying from the depths of my soul... Mourn, lament, hurt, wound, pain, sadden, make sorrowful, distress, and regret. "I have laid this on you daughter, to bear witness of my sorrow for the world...I hurt...You shall not bare this alone daughter, but I shall bare it with you... You are my beloved" ...

My heart, in general, was hurting from brokenness and I remember telling the Lord, I can't imagine how He feels with everyone around the globe that has broken His heart. In fact, on June 15th, 2020, I made note of this hurt. (Though it occurred on June 14th.) The second documentary: "I received a word of confirmation from my mother concerning the hurt I was feeling. Last week, I told the Lord something like, I can't imagine how He feels when people reject the love He gives (It was something to that effect). She confirmed after prayer, what I was feeling was for my ministry and that He's allowing me to feel what He feels (It's painful). This love was unexpected. It was the unconditional love of God."

That little touch of hurt felt like it could've crushed my heart. I wish I could delineate what I was experiencing. The Lord has given me such a sensitivity in the spirit. He'll let me know when He's not pleased and when something hurts Him. I too, weep when His presence is in the room. I remember being sensitive as a young girl. Even when I wasn't saved, I could feel Him.

I'm sharing this because when you're truly connected as a child of God, the Lord will share secrets with you. He'll allow you to see and sense things in the spirit realm. God will tell you to declare things the world will NOT want to hear. It can make you feel as though the world is against you. But know this, James 4:4 declares, "Ye adulterers and adulteresses, know ye not that the friendship of the world is enmity with God? Whosoever therefore will be a friend of the world is the enemy of God." So, it IS me against the world, but it's because of who HE IS INSIDE OF ME! But wait single mothers. There's hope! Jesus declares to us in John 16:33, "These things I have spoken unto you, that in me ye might have peace. In the world ye shall have tribulation: but be of good cheer; I have overcome the world."

Single mothers, because we aren't a friend of the world, it will be a challenge, especially with trivial things the world teaches. We'll be hated! I know it sounds harsh, but Jesus warned us about this. The Bible declares in John 15:18-19, "If the world hate you, ye know that it hated me before it hated you. If ye were of the world, the world would love HIS OWN: but because ye are NOT of the world, but I have CHOOSEN you out of the world, therefore the world hateth you."

Let it be known single mothers, we can't befriend the world or we become God's enemy. It's a challenge because we are in the world, but once in Christ, we're not of it. Look at the world around us. There's so much spoken AGAINST our Creator. The things we teach our children, will be looked down upon by the world. But don't compromise. Keep going! Turmoil and trouble are across the globe, so why become a comrade? I KNOW, John 3:16, "For God so loved the world, that he gave his only begotten Son, that whosoever believeth in him should not perish, but have everlasting life." But you can't stop there. Read the next verse, 17, "For God sent not his Son into the world to condemn the world; BUT THAT THE WORLD THROUGH HIM MIGHT BE SAVED."

He knew the world needed SAVING! Otherwise, they remain an enemy without salvation. It's vital we don't hand our children over to the world, so they might not be consumed. Though there's a mission in raising our children upon the foundation of the Word of God, we are surrounded by the world's thoughts, opinions, standards, etc. Though it's us against the world because of who HE IS, let's remember it's for HIS NAME'S SAKE and not our own. We win because HE already won! The Lord has already OVERCOME the world!

Parent in the Gap

Remember I stated in Challenge # 3, "When you become a covering to your children, you set up God's divine hedge of protection! You're signaling to the adversary that beyond THIS POINT, you're blocked! Why? Because you've APPLIED the blood of Jesus! Prayer has been your weapon!" This is the same concept, with where I'm going. Have you ever wondered why different ones in the Bible, before they became great, had a certain protocol? For example, their names were specified. There were things they couldn't do, eat or engage in.

Sampson's mother was told specifics. Judges 13:14 declares, "She may not eat of any thing that cometh of the vine, neither let her drink wine or strong drink, nor eat any unclean thing: all that I commanded her let her observe." Sampson's journey of specification began with his mother. Carried over to when he became a man and told all his heart to Delilah. Judges 16:17 declares, "That he told her all his heart, and said unto her, There hath not come a razor upon mine head; for I have been a Nazarite unto God from my MOTHER'S WOMB: if I be shaven, then my strength will go from me, and I shall become weak, and be like any other man."

Daniel, Shadrach, Meshach, and Abednego stood on their specifications as well. They were children with no blemishes, favored, skillful in all wisdom, cunning in knowledge, and understanding in science. They had purpose! Daniel 1:8 declares, "But Daniel PUPOSED in his heart that he would NOT defile himself with the portion of the King's meat, nor with wine which he drank: therefore he requested of the prince of the eunuchs that he might not defile himself." Verse 12, Daniel boldly says, "Prove thy servants, I beseech thee, ten days; and let them give us pulse to eat, and water to drink."

Or how about David, who mourned for his son Absalom when he died? Though his son was set out against his own father. David loved him so that he wanted the life of his son spared. Even to the point of wanting to die in his stead. 2 Samuel 18:33 declares, "And the king was much moved, and went up to the chamber over the gate, and wept: and as he went, thus he said O my son Absalom, my son Absalom, my son, my son Absalom! Would God I had died for thee, O Absalom, my son, my son!"

What are you saying this time woman of God? There's a protocol we too should follow in standing in the gap for our children. There are sacrifices made! Naturally so, standing in the gap can be defined as exposing oneself for the protection of another, defense against any assailing danger. Spiritually, we use prayer, the Word of God, praise and worship as our weapons of warfare!

2 Corinthians 10:4-5 declares, "(For the weapons of our warfare are not carnal, but mighty through God to the pulling down of strong holds;) Casting down imaginations, and every high thing that exalteth itself against the knowledge of God, and bringing into captivity every thought to the obedience of Christ;" Single mothers, we have to be the intercessors for our children and like Nehemiah, who didn't come down off the wall, though there was opposition! He kept building! There will be friction as we keep standing in the gap for our babies, but like a forcefield in the Spirit, we must guard them!

Let's explore these scriptures. Nehemiah 4:7-9 declares, "But it came to pass, that when Sanballat, and Tobiah, and the Arabians, and the Ammonites, and the Ashdodites, heard that the walls of Jerusalem were made up, and that the breaches began to be stopped, then they were very wroth, And conspired all of them together to come and to fight against Jerusalem, and to hinder it. Nevertheless we made our prayer unto our God, and set a watch against them day and night, because of them."

Like we see in the scripture, the enemy comes to try and conspire against what we've already tried to build with our hands and instill in our children. Imagine, you've built up the Word of God in them, the right morals, built on their character, standards etc. Then here comes the adversary, furious with what you're building, comes to fight and hinder what you've manufactured and constructed! The devil is a liar!

Continuing to verse 15, "And it came to pass, when our enemies heard that it was known unto us, and God had brought their counsel to nought, that we returned all of us to the wall, every one unto his work." Notice how God didn't allow Nehemiah's enemies to prosper. God brought their plan to NOUGHT and he and others CONTINUED their work in building the wall. So likewise, with us single mothers. The enemy will come at different seasons of our lives to deter us from what we're building. But with the proper spiritual weapons and being equipped, the enemy is no match! God will not allow him to take us out if you've put in the work. I truly believe what we've planted in our children is not in vain.

In my finishing, verses 19-21 declares, "And I said unto the nobles, and to the rulers, and to the rest of the people, The work is great and large, and we are separated upon the wall, one far from another. In what place therefore ye hear the trumpet, resort ye thither unto us: our God SHALL fight for us." So we laboured in the work: and half of them held the spears from the rising of the morning till the stars appeared."

Single mothers know you have a weapon in your hand, on deck. Though we might have different parts of the wall to cover, and we may be far apart from one another, we can still come together in the name of our Lord Jesus! As we stand in the gap for our seed, let us do the work the Lord has assigned to our hands. According to scripture, the Lord WILL fight for us! Do you believe it? He shall sis! Remain in good standing with God and do all you know for your children, according to the Word of God. Just as sure as we stand in the gap for our children, God will cover the rest of it!

Don't be afraid to stand therefore! Here's what you and I must do. According to Ephesians 6:13-20, it declares, "Wherefore take unto you the whole armour of God, that ye may be able to withstand in the evil day, and having done all to stand. Stand therefore, having your loins girt about with truth, and having on the breastplate of righteousness; And your feet shod with the preparation of the gospel of peace; Above all, taking the shield of faith, wherewith ye shall be able to quench all the fiery darts of the wicked. And take the helmet of salvation, and the sword of the Spirit, which is the word of God: Praying always with all prayer and supplication in the Spirit, and watching thereunto with all perseverance and supplication for all saints; And for me, that I may open my mouth boldly, to make known the mystery of the gospel, For which I am an ambassador in bonds: that therein I may speak boldly, as I ought to speak."

Let's suit up and stand in the gap! We have what we need if we follow suit!

Do You Love Them?

Oh, how we should cherish our seed that the Lord has given us. Who they become and how they develop truly matters. Goes back to the nurturing of the seed! It's easy for us to say we love our children, yet I realize we seem to withhold correction from the child. We're wrong! Whether a child wants to hear it or not, correction MUST be set in stone! This new generation of youngsters seem to struggle when it comes to parents giving them instruction. They cringe at it and always seem to have something to say. They want to do what they want when they want. They can't stand the truth...Not so!

What I won't say is the absence of a father is an excuse for why children struggle to obey. Consistent discipline in love is simply the answer! What I will say is it's a challenge as a single mom, or in a single parent home. There's something about the authority God has given to the man, who's supposed to be the head of the household. However, women can manage with instruction from the heavenly Father. We too, have authority!

So, what does the Bible have to say about correction single mothers? Proverbs 23:12-14 declares, "Apply thine heart unto instruction, and thine ears to the words of knowledge. Withhold not correction from the child: for if thou beatest him with the rod, he shall NOT die. Thou shalt beat him with the rod, and shalt deliver his soul from hell."

Wow! The Word of God is POWERFUL all by itself! Now when you talk about a rod, we're talking about a stick, switch, staff, etc. The Bible is clear. If we beat our children (which is a form of discipline), they will

NOT die and we're delivering their souls from hell. This also directs me to Proverbs 22:15, which declares, "Foolishness is bound in the heart of a child; BUT the rod of correction shall drive it far from him." Society won't speak of these things because today, it's easy to consider it abuse. My mother made a great illustration concerning law enforcement.

A. They can utilize a club and hit you.
B. They can taser you.
C. Or far worse, they can shoot you!

I'd rather be the one to discipline my child in love and teach them according to the ways of the Lord before anyone else. I'm young, but old school! All we've done in this "new age" is hinder our children. Where's the help? Why aren't we teaching and training them up? We've dealt away with the old path and adopted this "new way."

Has anybody noticed it's not working? Sure, each child is different, but if we love them, we'll discipline them! A spirit of rebellion and disobedience is after our children. Never have I seen such a difficult generation who won't take heed to sound doctrine! Not too many parents hit on this subject, but I will! Are we still following?

2 Timothy 3:1-2 declares, "This know also, that in the LAST DAYS perilous times shall come, For men will be lovers of their own selves, covetous, boasters, proud, blasphemers, disobedient to parents, unthankful, unholy" ... These perilous times are already here single mothers! How many times will we see shooting after shooting at school, suicidal tragedies, bullying and even worse, quarrelsome issues in the household and children killing their parents?

It starts IN the home! We don't want to be brought into open shame. Proverbs 29:15 tells us sis, "The rod and reproof give wisdom: But a child left to himself bringeth his MOTHER to shame." Did you notice how it said "mother?" Shame is defined as a painful feeling of humiliation or distress caused by wrong or foolish behavior. Embarrassment, shamefacedness! It's as if your child is a reflection of you and they are. When they're in trouble, it's going to be brought to us. It's a domino effect! Though they will reap the consequences of THEIR choices, we'll be living with the after math of knowing, "That's my child."

Do we love them enough? Hebrews 12:6 declares, "For whom the Lord loveth he chasteneth, And scourgeth every son whom he receiveth." Likewise, this scripture applies to us and our seed. We must chasten them! Proverbs 13:24 is an eye opener as well. It declares, "He that spareth his rod hateth his son: But he that loveth him chasteneth him betimes." Betimes, meaning early, speedily and occasionally. It's necessary! These are the challenges we must face in today's society.

I will also say everything is not a beating, but rather stern reminders. It depends on what the child did. I've had to learn this in raising my seed. Great instruction with wisdom is needed. Might I also add, stop trying to be a friend to your children. Sure, have a close bond and relationship with them, but there should always be a level of respect and boundaries set in place.

Parents can do certain things which friends can't! This is controversial also, but you should understand there's a reason God gave us the title "PARENT." We have a level of authority walking in that. Don't forget it! By no means am I saying mishandle your authority. We don't want to be misguided but do it with wisdom! Too many parents in this new age are trying to befriend their children and so there's a misunderstanding along with confusion. Our children are supposed to honor and obey. The Lord didn't put an age limit on it either! (See Exodus 20:12 and Ephesians 6:2)

For example, have you ever seen adults talk to their elderly parents with disrespect? I have many times! It's out of order, even though their child has reached adulthood. It sounds and looks awful! If we could only see...

I challenge us single mothers...Ask yourself, "Do I love my child?" There are times we must explain to them the reasons for discipline and get them to understand because we love them, it must be done. They may not always agree, but that's ok. As a child looking back, I understand why my mother did what she did. Because I was a child at the time, I didn't understand the fullness of discipline. Our children can't see what we see! Nine times out of ten, they aren't looking at the bigger picture and may miss the concept. 1 Corinthians 13:11 declares, "When I was a child, I spake as a child, I understood as a child, I thought as a child: but when I became a man, I put away childish things."

This goes back to the accountability that the Father will hold us to. Because it's in His Word, we must adhere to it. If we love them, we'll follow through!

Closing Remarks

Single mothers, I hope I've said something within these 11 chapters that have helped build you. It was the will of God that I am obedient and write this book. To those that have followed me with all three books, thank you so much! I'm hoping you can see my growth and what the Lord is doing in me! As I take this adventure to be not JUST a writer, but a scribe for the Kingdom of God, I pray the Father will continue to anoint me to do His will concerning it. Be strong and of good courage and know we never walk this journey alone, but with Christ! Every challenge we face gives us an opportunity for growth!

I asked the Lord if there was anything He wanted the single mothers to know and if so, what would He want to say. I believe He placed these words in my spirit. "I see and I know your worth...Many have tried to trample them under their feet" ...I believe He wanted me to remind you of this scripture: Matthew 7:6 declares, "Give not that which is holy unto the dogs, neither cast ye your pearls before swine, lest they trample them under their feet, and turn again and rend you" ...

I love you with the love of Christ! Be the mother you've been called and chosen to be! Blessings and To God Be the Glory for this series of books, until the next time, God willing!

"Every wise woman buildeth her house: But the foolish plucketh it down with her hands (Proverbs 14:1)." Let's build together!

Sincerely,
Tréasa Brown

About The Author

Prophetess Tréasa Brown was born and raised in Colorado and is from a little city called Boulder. She's the 3rd child of 4 children and was dedicated back to the Lord as a child. Prophetess Brown was raised in the fear and admonition of the Lord and is a God-fearing woman as a result. The Lord saved her in January of 2012, and she was filled with the Holy Ghost on March 28th of 2012. Prophetess Brown was baptized in April of 2016 under Brian Carn Ministries and that same year, she was baptized by her former Pastor, Superintendent Charles E. Scurles. Prophetess Brown once served as a secretary in the Young Women's Christian Counsel. She was a Primary Sunday School Teacher, Local District Sunshine Band Leader, Bible

Band Teacher, Assistant Coordinator for the Young Women of Excellence, a Praise and Worship Leader and has preached the Gospel. As a Leader, Prophetess Tréasa Brown is currently serving under the leadership of Overseer/Pastor Larry Herron and Co-Pastor/First Lady Herron at DJIC Ministries, which stands for Deliverance Jesus Is Coming. As a woman of God, she loves spending time in the presence of God, and she is a prayer warrior and intercessor. Prayer is her passion! Prophetess Brown was destined to be a writer and an author and she has currently written 2 books by the instruction of Almighty God titled, "Single Mother's and Living for Christ and Single Mothers and Living for Christ 2." She also Co-Authored a book called "I Almost Died," with Prophetess Kimberly Moses and 7 other Co-Authors. She's been a journalist for 10 years, writing prophetically while hearing, learning, and studying the voice of God. Prophetess Brown enjoys encouraging others and is drawn to the brokenhearted. The Lord has called her to the nations, the prophetic ministry and to the office of the prophet. Prophetess Brown is yet to be birthed in the healing and deliverance ministry and the Lord is raising her up for His Glory! She has a hunger and a thirst for the things of God and her desire is to please the Father so that He may get ALL the Glory out of her life! She's excited about what He is going to do as her ministry is birthed! To God Be the Glory!

Index

A

D